CW00541296

SHAKESPEARE's SISTER

BY EMMA WHIPDAY

SERVING THEATRE

SINCE 1830

WWW.SAMUELFRENCH.CO.UK
WWW.SAMUELFRENCH.COM

FOR AMATEUR PRODUCTION ENQUIRIES

UNITED KINGDOM AND WORLD EXCLUDING NORTH AMERICA
plays@SamuelFrench-London.co.uk
020 7255 4302/01

UNITED STATES AND CANADA
info@SamuelFrench.com
1-866-598-8449

Each title is subject to availability from Samuel French, depending upon country of performance.

Shakespeare's Sister was first performed as a staged reading at the Theatre Royal Haymarket as part of the Theatre Royal Haymarket Masterclass Trust's Pitch Your Play scheme, supported by the Noël Coward Foundation and the Vernon Charitable Trust, September 2015.

CAST

(in order of appearance)

JUDITH SHAKESPEARE	Remmie Milner
DOROTHY CLAYTON/SUSANNAH	Beth Eyre
LUCY MORGAN/HAMNET	Roseanna Brear
WILLIAM UNDERHILL/PHILIP HENSLOWE/SOLDIER 2	Simon Blake
JOHN SHAKESPEARE/SERGEANT	Andy Murton
MARY SHAKESPEARE	Clare Bloomer
NED ALLEYN	Dino Kelly
DICK BURBAGE	George Johnston
WILL SHAKESPEARE	Mike Evans
JOAN HENSLOWE	Simona Bitmaté
AUGUSTINE PHILLIPS	Joseph Dawson
THOMAS EGERTON/SOLDIER 1	Tim Harker
NARRATOR	Brian McMahon

Creative team

DIRECTOR	Asia Osborne
PRODUCER	James Marsden
LIGHTING	Andy Peregrine
MUSIC	Sam Brown

This production was revived for the King's College London Shakespeare Festival, 'What You Will', as part of the Shakespeare400 celebrations, February 2016. James Law joined the original cast as William Underhill/Philip Henslowe/Soldier 2.

To my parents,
with love,

and

in memory of
Emily Stiff.

AUTHOR'S NOTE

"Let me imagine, since the facts are so hard to come by,
what would have happened had Shakespeare had a wonderfully gifted
sister, called Judith, let us say."

Virginia Woolf, *A Room of One's Own*

This is not a true story.

The Judith Shakespeare that appears in these pages did not exist. Shakespeare did have a sister, called Joan; she married a hatter, and lived out her life in Stratford-upon-Avon. To our knowledge, she never wrote a play. *Shakespeare's Sister* imagines what might have happened if she had.

When Woolf invented a brief history of Judith Shakespeare in *A Room of One's Own*, she suggested that it would have been impossible for any woman to write the plays of Shakespeare in the age of Shakespeare. Woolf's Judith ran away to London, aged sixteen, to write plays, but the men of the theatre laughed in her face. She had an affair with actor-manager Nick Greene, became pregnant by him, and killed herself.

I want to tell a very different tale about Judith Shakespeare. My play does not show that a poet's heart is incompatible with a woman's body, and it does not suggest that for a woman, sex and death must go together. Instead, I explore how it would have been impossible for a woman to write the plays of Shakespeare in the age of Shakespeare, because of the familial, societal, economic and political pressures that shaped her world. I also want to challenge the isolation of Woolf's female playwright – more than one woman may have wanted to make plays in Elizabethan England, and more than one man may have been willing to help her.

This play reimagines the life of a canonical writer from the perspective of those who were forbidden the roles of actor and writer: the women who lived on the edge of the world of the theatre, but couldn't inhabit it. My play is populated with characters an Elizabethan actor would have recognised: Edward Alleyn, Richard Burbage, Philip Henslowe, his step-daughter Joan, Lucy Morgan, Dorothy Clayton, Augustine Phillips and Thomas Egerton all existed, though I've taken some liberties with dates and circumstances. In peopling Elizabethan London with the names and personalities that walked its streets, I've tried to bring to life the rich, dirty, and astonishing world of early modern theatre-makers. I've also tried to suggest some of the ways in which the challenges they faced resonate with the London we know today: Judith and the players face unemployment and debt in a plague-ridden economic depression, in a sexist society where women are freely objectified and their freedoms are curtailed, under a government battling religious extremism in a climate of fear and suspicion. The liberties I have taken, and the stories I have told, are my own.

Like Judith, I have found that a play can be dreamed up alone, but it can only come to life with the help of others. Among those others, I must thank Hazel Kerr, Blayne George, Josh Brown and Kezia Newson at Masterclass, along with the Theatre Royal Haymarket, the Noël Coward Foundation and the Vernon Charitable Trust, for making the staged reading of this play possible. I must also thank Asia Osborne and Brian McMahon, for brilliance, encouragement and dreaming with me from the very beginning; James Marsden for joining our pitching team; and all the cast and creative team for being utterly wonderful. Thanks to my colleagues at King's, and particularly Gordon McMullan for including my play in the Shakespeare400 celebrations; to Sarah Wolf and Felicity Barks at Samuel French; to Penny Woolcock (and the support of the Arvon Foundation) for the advice that shaped this play; to Oskar Cox Jensen, for reading, re-reading and writing by my side; and to my friends and family, too many to name, for their support. A play can only be made together with a community of friends and collaborators, and I have been very lucky in mine.

Emma Whipday
February 2016

AUTHOR'S BIOGRAPHY

Emma Whipday is a Teaching Fellow in Shakespeare and Early Modern English Literature at King's College London. She is also a Globe Education Lecturer at Shakespeare's Globe. Emma studied English at Oxford, and has received an MA and PhD in Shakespeare from University College London (UCL). She has taught at UCL; Brasenose College, Oxford; and the Royal Central School of Speech and Drama.

Emma is a winner of the Masterclass 2015 'Pitch Your Play' competition. She is an Associate Writer for Oxford-based theatre company Reverend Productions, which has staged her adaptations of classic novels at the Edinburgh Fringe and various Oxford colleges and gardens. Her short plays have been performed in the Old Vic Tunnels and at an Old Vic New Voices Showcase. *Shakespeare's Sister* is Emma's first original full-length play.

Emma has directed "practice as research" productions of Samuel Daniel's *The Tragedie of Cleopatra* and "The Tragedy of Merry" from *Two Lamentable Tragedies* at UCL. She has run workshops on early modern drama at the Wellcome Collection, the London Renaissance Seminar, the Huntington Library in California and the Shakespeare400 Festival at King's College London; and has given public lectures at Shakespeare's Globe, Knole House for the National Trust, TEDx at Goodenough College, Somerville College Chapel and UCL. Emma has spoken about her research on BBC Radio Oxford, and has published articles in academic journals and essay collections on: Elizabethan domestic murder; domestic tragedy; 'practice as research'; and the RSC 2014 'Roaring Girls' season.

CHARACTERS

(in order of appearance)

JUDITH SHAKESPEARE, 19
Judith is bright, talented, impetuous and intense.

SUSANNAH SHAKESPEARE, 9
Susannah is precocious and affectionate
(can be doubled with Dorothy).

HAMNET SHAKESPEARE, 6
Hamnet is sweet and naïve (can be doubled with Lucy).

AUGUSTINE PHILLIPS ('PHIL'), mid 20s
Phil is laddish, calculating and self-interested.

EDWARD ALLEYN ('NED'), 26
Ned is a charismatic and successful actor.

WILLIAM UNDERHILL, early 40s
William is steady, successful and well off. Warwickshire burr.

JOHN SHAKESPEARE, 50s
John is husband to Mary and father to Judith and Will; he is a
handsome, popular, confident man gone to seed.

MARY SHAKESPEARE, 50s
Mary is wife to John and mother to Judith and Will; she is an intelligent
and affectionate woman, but poverty and loss of stability have worn her
down.

RICHARD BURBAGE ('DICK'), early 20s
Richard is talented and engaging, but with a teenage rebelliousness.
Cockney accent.

WILL SHAKESPEARE, 26
Will is ambitious and brilliant, but has not yet achieved the success or
recognition he dreams of.

PHILLIP HENSLOWE ('HENSLOWE'), early 40s
Henslowe is a theatre manager, brothel owner and impresario, and a
prosperous and canny man. Cockney accent.

JOAN HENSLOWE, early 20s
Joan is Henslowe's daughter; she is reserved and sharp, but passionate
and protective. Cockney accent.

LUCY MORGAN, late teens
Lucy is affectionate, vain, sweet and seems very young. Cockney accent.

DOROTHY CLAYTON, early 30s

Dorothy is a cross-dressing woman with charisma and physical power. Cockney accent.

SERGEANT

A self-important petty thug (can be doubled with John). Cockney accent.

SOLDIER 1

Taciturn and violent (can be doubled with Egerton). Cockney accent.

SOLDIER 2

A complacent bully (can be doubled with Henslowe).

THOMAS EGERTON ('EGERTON'), 40s

Chivalrous, powerful, secret, a gentleman.

JAILOR

Dutiful and compassionate (can be doubled with Ned). Cockney accent.

ACT ONE

Early Summer, 1592. **JOHN SHAKESPEARE**'s *house, Stratford.*

It is a substantial house, but with the faded and makeshift air of gradual poverty. We are in a room at the front of the house. Upstage, a door and window open to the street beyond.

The furniture is sparse, but all is neat and clean. A pot hangs in the fireplace, stage right.

JUDITH SHAKESPEARE *sits on the floor, an inkpot and a pile of ink-splattered pages at her side, more pages resting in her lap. She scribbles with energy.*

JUDITH *(in a low voice)* Must I go alone? No – would you send me there alone? I will, my child – no – I must.

A face appears at the window. It is **SUSANNAH**.

SUSANNAH What are you writing?

JUDITH *moves to cover the pages, but knocks the inkpot with her hand.*

JUDITH Oh!

She rights it almost instantly, but the damage is done – her hands are stained, and her dress is spotted. She dabs with her handkerchief.

The face at the window disappears. Enter **SUSANNAH**, *contrite, through the front door.*

1

SUSANNAH Oh, Aunt Judith – it will wash clean, I am sure!

JUDITH Susannah, my sweet, you must try not to surprise so –

SUSANNAH Oh, do not preach, Aunty, I have enough of that from Mama. Are you writing to Father?

JUDITH I have no need. The players passed through Canterbury Thursday last, your Grandpa said – they should be here by the morrow.

SUSANNAH They did not come last summer.

JUDITH Last summer there was no plague. This year the players are driven from the city, your father with them – driven to us! He will come soon, little one.

A face appears at the window. It is **HAMNET**.

SUSANNAH Is that your play?

JUDITH Hush! Do not speak of it so loud.

SUSANNAH But is it?

HAMNET *(from the window)* Mama says plays are unmoral.

JUDITH Hamnet, my dear, you must not –

Enter **HAMNET**, *not at all contrite, through the front door.*

HAMNET Why are all plays unmoral?

JUDITH *(gathering up her pages)* It's immoral, Hamnet.

HAMNET Aunt Judith, what's immoral?

JUDITH It means something God does not like.

HAMNET Then God does not like plays.

JUDITH Of course he does –

HAMNET But they are unmoral –

SUSANNAH Immoral, Hamnet –

HAMNET You didn't know that –

SUSANNAH I did indeed –

HAMNET You didn't once correct me –

JUDITH Come, come, you two!

HAMNET But she –

SUSANNAH But I –

JUDITH Shall I tell your papa you are ill-mannered when he comes?

HAMNET Papa?

> **JUDITH** *eases up a floorboard, and hides the quill, ink, and papers beneath.*

SUSANNAH I did not know of that.

JUDITH And if you would continue not to know, Susannah, I should be greatly obliged.

HAMNET Truly – Papa?

SUSANNAH Yes, Hamnet. Oh, I do like a secret –

HAMNET I do not believe in Papa.

SUSANNAH Don't be silly, Hamnet.

JUDITH Why not, chuck?

HAMNET I have never seen him.

SUSANNAH Of course you have.

JUDITH Do you not recall? It is two summers since – but he stayed for above a month. He would dandle you upon his knee –

HAMNET I do not believe it.

SUSANNAH Well, you shall, Hamnet, for you shall see him.

JUDITH He should be crossing the hills as we speak, in a cart full of players.

HAMNET Truly?

JUDITH Truly.

Trumpets sound, from afar.

Did you hear that?

SUSANNAH Is it the players? Have they come?

Trumpets again, and drums.

He is here! He is here!

The children dash to the door. Exit **SUSANNAH** *and* **HAMNET**.

JUDITH *runs to the window, and leans out.*

JUDITH Do you see them, Susannah? Do you see them?

SUSANNAH *(off)* They are coming! Oh, the colours! They are throwing their hats!

Trumpets and drums, even louder.

PHIL *(off)* Lord Strange's Men are here! Bid a Stratford welcome to the players of Lord Strange!

JUDITH Is he with them? Has he come?

SUSANNAH *(off)* I cannot see him –

HAMNET *(off)* Papa? Papa?

JUDITH *leans from the window.*

JUDITH Sirs! Excuse me, sirs! Is my brother with you?

NED *(off)* Who is your brother, fair one?

JUDITH William Shakespeare.

NED *(off)* In London!

JUDITH *climbs slowly down from the window, and sits.*

Enter SUSANNAH *and* HAMNET, *crestfallen.*

SUSANNAH You said he would come.

HAMNET I do not care if I see him.

SUSANNAH Nor do I. I do not care in the slightest.

JUDITH I am sure he has sent word – I will ask the players myself. Go tell your mama that.

SUSANNAH Must we go?

JUDITH Yes, Susannah, you must. But if you care to, meet me at the townhouse after – the players play this afternoon, and the first performance will be the Mayor's treat.

HAMNET May I come, too? Please may I?

JUDITH Ask your mama. Home, now.

SUSANNAH I thought he would come.

JUDITH As did I. See you at the townhouse, chucks.

Exit SUSANNAH *and* HAMNET. JUDITH, *troubled, tidies her hair and fetches her shawl.*

A knock at the door. JUDITH *goes to it.*

WILLIAM UNDERHIILL *is at the door.*

WILLIAM Good afternoon, mistress –

JUDITH Oh. William. Good afternoon. I'm just heading out, I'm afraid –

WILLIAM Could you stop a moment? Your father was good enough to invite me to supper –

JUDITH Was he, indeed? Well, I'm afraid there's little enough – it seems he was not good enough to inform me –

WILLIAM I've a brace of pheasants with me. It would give me pleasure to offer them for your table.

JUDITH That's very good of you, William. Now, if you'll excuse me –

WILLIAM Perhaps I might keep you a little longer – will you let me come in a moment?

JUDITH I am alone in the house.

WILLIAM Your father said I might join you.

JUDITH Oh indeed?

WILLIAM I suppose he thought, as an old friend of the family –

JUDITH Well, come in, come in. We must not expose ourselves to gossip on the doorstep.

Enter **WILLIAM**, *with his pheasants.*

WILLIAM I rather hoped that might not be a problem.

JUDITH Whatever do you mean? I mean no offence by my hurry, it's simply that –

WILLIAM *(clasping her hand)* No offence, Judith. Quite the opposite, in fact. Oh, I did not mean to come to it so quickly – I had hoped to make it elegant –

JUDITH Master Underhill, you forget yourself.

She tries to extricate her hand, but he holds it fast.

WILLIAM Indeed, I do not. I have been wanting to ask you this long while – and I have your father's permission –

JUDITH *(icy)* Permission to do what, exactly?

WILLIAM To take you as my wife.

JUDITH I see.

WILLIAM Oh dear, I have put it clumsily, I know.

JUDITH Well, Master Underhill, you may have my father's permission to take me as your wife, but unfortunately, that will not answer, for you do not have mine.

WILLIAM Let me begin again –

JUDITH It seems to me quite clear. You wish to marry me. My father wishes you to marry me. I, however, do not wish you to marry me, and so we come to an end. Now, I must go about my errands –

She makes for the door. He slams his arm against it so she cannot open it, and bars her way with his body.

WILLIAM Your errands can wait, Judith.

JUDITH Master Underhill –

WILLIAM I am offering you my heart, my body, and my wealth. My fortune may not be great, but I am willing to give you all I have. Your father's debts to me are considerable, and they have crippled him – have crippled you all. I offer to cancel them. I will forget your pitiful marriage portion –

JUDITH You think that this is the way to my heart?

WILLIAM You love your family, girl – do you not? I will provide for them, and for you, Judith. You will never want. We will work hard, but we will eat well and sleep without worry.

JUDITH You would do better with a girl with a portion and no debts behind her, to secure such a future. I cannot think why you have chosen me to share in this happy fate.

WILLIAM Can you not, Judith? I have cared for you ever since you skipped into my orchard to steal my apples.

JUDITH I did not go to steal –

WILLIAM I have not forgot it, Judith. I have waited, and now I am come to ask for your hand. Will you give it me, for friendship?

JUDITH I will give no man my hand for friendship. The good Lord ordained marriage for love, and I will give my hand when love asks for it.

WILLIAM Our Lord ordained marriage for help, for comfort, and for children, Judith, and all those I offer. I am not as ready with the words as you young folk are, but I admit I have a certain – fondness for you. *(Taking her hand again)* Come, I will say the word if you bid me –

JUDITH *(gentler now)* No, William. I would not have you say it. You have said enough, and I am thankful for the offer, truly I am. You are a good man. But my answer must still be no, and now, I bid you good day.

WILLIAM Your father will expect you to await his coming, Miss Shakespeare. It is not only your own fate you answer for here.

JUDITH Indeed it is not. What do your children say to the match? Do they seek a new mother? What of your late wife?

WILLIAM My wife, God rest her soul, is dead and buried, and I've a duty to wed again. My children need no new mother, for they're near enough grown, but a woman's touch never did a household harm. Let us sit and await your father, my dear.

JUDITH It is a good while until supper time, Master Underhill. I suggest you wait elsewhere.

*Enter **JOHN SHAKESPEARE**, to see **WILLIAM** still grasping **JUDITH**'s hand.*

JOHN Ah! Just as I'd hoped. The love birds are cooing together pleasantly, I see?

WILLIAM *drops her hand.*

WILLIAM Not so, Goodman Shakespeare. Your daughter has refused me.

JOHN My Judith? My girl refuse *you*, Master Underhill? Come, you must be mistaken –

JUDITH He is not, Father. I have refused him.

JOHN Now, girl, do not disgrace me –

JUDITH I intend no disgrace, Father. But I cannot accept him.

JOHN Is William not rich enough for you? Not sure enough? Is he not a good man?

JUDITH A good man, and a kind one. You know that I respect him –

JOHN You can show your respect, girl, by wedding him! Do you care nothing for this family? For poor Anne and the chicks your brother has all but abandoned? Must all my children go against me, and bring disgrace to our name?

JUDITH I would not go against you, Father.

JOHN Then obey me in this. Accept Master Underhill. I command you.

JUDITH (*very softly*) No.

WILLIAM I will hear no more of this. I am a proud man, Goodman Shakespeare, as you know, and this is beyond –

Enter **MARY SHAKESPEARE**.

MARY Why, what is the matter here? Good day to you, Master Underhill. Husband, are you well?

JOHN Wife, we are bereft. We have no children.

MARY Fie, John, you embarrass Master Underhill. Will you join us for supper, sir?

WILLIAM Forgive me, Goodwife Shakespeare.

MARY What a pity! But I hope we may meet again soon.

WILLIAM I do not think so. I pray I may never enter this house again – no, not if no others were open to me. Good day to you all.

Exit **WILLIAM**, *slamming the door behind him.*

MARY *(moving to the pot)* Why, what has happened here? How have you offended poor William? Judith, you have let this stew spoil. I did not bring you up for a slattern. And look to your hair, you must tidy yourself. Well, John?

> **MARY** *pours water from a pitcher into the stew, and busies herself about the room.*

JOHN Woman, I will tell you, if you take a moment's breath! This wench – this – this thing that I will not own –

MARY John!

JOHN She has refused him. Our impudent hussy has dared –

MARY John, I will not have you speak so. Tell me plainly, now.

JUDITH Master Underhill has proposed marriage to me, Mother.

MARY Has he, indeed? Well, that is rather forward –

JOHN I gave him permission, wife! The banns were all but read.

MARY And did not think to mention it? Not to Judith? Nor to her mother?

JOHN Woman, I am her father. She is mine to dispose of as I see fit.

MARY That's as may be, but our Judith has a will –

JOHN Don't I know it.

MARY She's too like her father in that.

JOHN Too like her brother. Oh, how have I misgoverned, to raise two rebels to my household?

MARY Calm yourself, John. Here, girl – stir this.

JUDITH *stirs the pot.* JOHN *spots her ink-stained hands.*

JOHN *(dangerously quiet)* What's that on your hands, my girl?

JUDITH A spillage, Father.

JOHN A spillage *of what?*

MARY Now, John –

JOHN Come here, girl. Come. Show.

She goes to him, holds out her hands.

Is that ink I see? How came it to be there?

JUDITH I spilled it, Father. I was writing.

MARY Oh, Judith –

JOHN *What* were you writing?

JUDITH *(very softly)* A play.

JOHN Show me.

JUDITH Father, I –

JOHN Show me your scribblings.

She goes to the floorboard, lifts it, takes out the pages.

JUDITH Here, Father.

JOHN And you hid them here? Under my very nose? Why?

JUDITH I thought you would not approve.

JOHN So it is for this that you neglect your house affairs. This is the vanity that makes you refuse good men – this is the foolishness that has you disobey your father – well, I will not have it. I will not have it in my house, daughter – no, I will not!

He snatches the pages from her, then raises his hand to strike –

MARY John, no.

JOHN Spare the rod, spoil the child.

JUDITH Papa, please!

He drags her by the hair to the fireplace, where he throws the pages on the fire. Some fall in and burn, but most are scattered about the floor.

JOHN Here is your work. Here is your place. Minding your family, not staining yourself with ink. I did not raise you to prostitute yourself to the pen. I raised none of my children so. Oh, did I labour and slave for this? Hey?

JUDITH *(weeping)* Papa, Papa. Forgive me, Papa.

JOHN You could have raised our family, girl. You could've saved us. Do you know how I strive to keep us from the mud? Eh? Eh?

JUDITH Papa.

JOHN Oh, I cannot look at you.

He goes to leave.

MARY Where do you go, John? Husband?

JOHN To the tavern.

MARY Your supper will spoil.

JOHN I have no stomach for it.

Exit **JOHN**, *slamming the door.*

MARY *(sighing)* Well, these things must mend themselves. I would not have you wed unhappily, Judith, but I wish you had managed it better. And as for the scribbling – it must end. Today. No good can come of it.

JUDITH Will says I have some skill –

MARY Your brother has left his family. You would do well to avoid his advice.

JUDITH He sends money when he can –

MARY He does not send himself. *(Of the pheasants)* Has Master Underhill left these? Well, I will take them along for Anne and the little ones. God knows they have need of them.

MARY turns to go.

JUDITH *(in a low voice)* I cannot marry him, Mother. I cannot.

MARY *(without looking at her)* Can you stay here to be a burden to us, Judith? To weigh us down when you could have saved us?

Exit MARY.

JUDITH dashes to the fire, rescues some pages, collects some from the floor. Then she breaks down into sobs. A face appears at the window. It is NED ALLEYN.

NED Anyone home?

Startled to hear a strange man's voice, JUDITH wipes her hands across her face and turns.

What ails you, sweet?

JUDITH Forgive me, sir, for my foolishness. I am quite well. Is it my father you seek?

NED Do you not remember me, honey? It was I told you your brother stops in London.

JUDITH Oh, you are with the players?

NED It is not often my face is so fast forgotten. But in this instance, I will forgive you.

JUDITH Do you have a message from my brother, sir?

NED I do indeed, fair one.

He passes it through the window. JUDITH reaches for it, but he pulls it back.

But may I not present it inside? The wind howls something fearful out here.

JUDITH Would you give me the letter? I may not invite you in.

NED's face disappears from the window. The door pushes open, and NED is there.

NED I am entrusted with the letter by your brother, my lady – *(pulling out a pouch)* and with this bag of coin. Will you not trust me also?

JUDITH We have not been introduced.

NED Permit me, then, to introduce myself. Edward Alleyn, at your service – Ned to my friends, of whom I hope you will be one. *(In mock seriousness)* You have twice offended my pride today, mistress – by forgetting my face, and by failing to attend our performance at the townhouse. Do not refuse my friendship also. It would break my heart.

JUDITH Very well, come, then – but quickly.

Enter NED.

May I have the letter now?

NED You may have letter and coin both.

He hands them over. She throws the money aside and tears open the letter.

As she reads, forgetful of him, NED glances about, sees the pages scattered on the floor. He picks one up, and begins to read.

JUDITH My brother is writing poetry – that is why he did not come. It seems he has found a patron – Henry someone – do you know him?

NED Hmmm? There are many Henrys... This is powerful stuff, Judith.

JUDITH Master Alleyn, you should not pry!

NED No, I like it. I do.

He prepares to declaim it.

NED *is agreed to be the greatest actor upon the Elizabethan stage. He reads* **JUDITH**'*s words with feeling, at first half-unconsciously, then with conscious pride.*

JUDITH*, at first embarrassed and ready to stop him, soon falls under the spell of his voice.*

You would not see me because you feared my chains still held you. They still do. This body, this body you took and used and loved, this body bound you to me, and so you had it locked away.

He breaks off.

Inelegant, perhaps, but powerful. Who is she?

JUDITH *(stiffly)* She is Vashti, a deposed queen. She speaks to her former lover, the king.

NED Ever had a former lover, Judith?

He is being provocative, but she answers him seriously.

JUDITH No. But I do not need to have had one to imagine how she feels.

NED And how does she feel?

JUDITH *(softly)* Lost. Angry and helpless and lost. And without hope.

NED What happens to her?

JUDITH She dies. Executed by the king.

NED A tragic end.

JUDITH Sometimes I think it must be simpler to make a good death than to live a good life.

NED But to die is the hardest thing there is. To leave it all behind, when life offers so much.

JUDITH Offers so much to you, perhaps. Life can be an eternal compromise. Duty and obedience and sacrifice –

NED Of whom are we speaking, mistress?

JUDITH Of Queen Vashti, of course. But the same applies to any girl who may not make her own way in the world – who must be at the mercy of the men that choose to love her.

NED Wise words, for one so young. But here I am talking sense to a pretty girl – a sad betrayal of my principles.

JUDITH Which are?

NED Why, to enjoy myself, if I can. To get pleasure out of life. And to only talk nonsense to beauty – it is the perfect homage.

JUDITH Must you always flirt?

NED Must you always be solemn?

JUDITH I feel rather solemn, just now.

NED Sweet, I do not know what your trouble is, but these pages are charred and your face is stained with tears, and a girl who can write such stuff as this would not weep for a torn gown or a lost thimble. I would help you, if I may.

JUDITH Thank you for your kind offer, Master Alleyn. But there is little you can do.

NED *(looking at the pages)* The play is finished, you say?

JUDITH All but. Some pages have been – have been lost, but it is almost complete.

NED Complete it, and send it to London. Master Henslowe has sent word that the plague has ended. The players are to be recalled. Playwrights are a remarkably short-lived lot, and the Rose Theatre is ever in search of new plays.

JUDITH Would you – would you be so kind as to take it to my brother? And ask him to sell it – on my behalf?

NED Why not take it yourself?

JUDITH You jest, Master Alleyn.

NED I do not. We ride to London at first light tomorrow. Join us.

JUDITH An unmarried woman, travelling alone with the players?

NED I would protect you, Judith.

JUDITH Would you?

NED But you are right, of course. Forgive me. I can be rash and unthinking – particularly where a lovely girl is concerned. It would be foolish – your reputation would never recover.

JUDITH There is nothing but sorrow and guilt for me here. Does it matter so much if I leave it all behind?

NED Judith, I am a jesting fool. It is far better –

JUDITH My father has betrothed me against my will, Master Alleyn. Would you stay, if it were your choice to make? Would you marry where you could not love?

NED There is no knowing what a man will do, if he must.

JUDITH And I will do what I must – I will go to my brother and sell my play. I will take you up on your offer, Master Alleyn. I will join your players, and to London.

NED If you are sure of this –

JUDITH I am.

NED But it must be at your own risk, mistress – I can take no responsibility for it.

JUDITH Why, Ned – where is your dashing courage now?

NED Quite diminished, in the face of yours, Judith. We ride at first light. Will you join us then?

JUDITH I cannot leave when I may be seen. I must go long before the sun rises.

NED Tonight, then?

JUDITH Tonight.

NED I will look for you, fair one. But I'll forgive you if you fail us.

He kisses her hand.

JUDITH I will be there.

Lights down.

ACT TWO

The Rose Theatre.

The theatre is closed. It is empty, dusty and bare.

RICHARD BURBAGE (DICK) *is centre stage. He is dusty and unkempt.*

He is attempting to throw wooden rings onto a small wooden stick. He often misses.

Enter **WILL SHAKESPEARE**. *He is neat and dapper, if a little frayed around the edges – a poor man's attempt at elegance. He watches* **DICK** *in silence for a moment.*

WILL You need to find yourself employment, Dick.

DICK *(without looking up)* I cannot.

WILL Cannot, or will not?

DICK The plague forbids all plays. I am a player. Ergo, no employment.

WILL When one's father owns two of the city's theatres, one is at an advantage even in plague.

DICK When one's father is a pus-swollen prick, and one refuses to grovel to him –

WILL And the companies touring the provinces? They have offended you also?

DICK I could put the same question to you, Master Shakespeare. Do the little towns not bid you welcome? Do your wife and children not look for you daily?

19

WILL I'm leaving the city, Dick.

DICK Good. Go home, Will. There's nothing for you here.

WILL I have received an invitation. To Whitley Lodge.

DICK To where?

WILL Whitley Lodge, near Titchfield, Hampshire.

DICK *(as if it is a foreign country)* Hampshire!

WILL The seat of the Earl of Southampton.

DICK That boy has bewitched you, William.

WILL He is my patron. He pays me.

DICK Pays you for what?

WILL For my verses, Richard. My poetry. Throughout these dead months, as playwrights have starved, as Greene has been abandoned even by his whore and his bastard, and Kyd's half-dead in the Tower for blasphemy –

DICK And every money-lender coins it while we fight to keep flesh on our bones. I know, Will. Times are hard.

WILL But I have not starved. My family has not starved.

DICK Thanks to your glove-maker father –

WILL No, Dick. It is my pen they must thank.

DICK And the Earl's generosity.

WILL The Earl is a generous man.

DICK Admit it, Will. You go not for the money nor for the family you never see. You go for the Earl's smiles and his pretty face, for velvet and lace and the right to wear a sword, you go in search of gentle status and in hope of glory. You go for the dream of poetry and the love of your Muse. If it was a living you wanted, you'd follow the players to the provinces, and see your wife on the journey. Go if you must, Will, but go honestly.

WILL God bless you, Dick, for I can get nothing past you. Here's hoping that the players return soon, and the Master of the Revels lets you play. But I cannot stay.

DICK Will not.

WILL I am to Titchfield, and not even you can stop me. When Ned returns, he should bring word from my family. Send it on to me.

DICK Your poor wife, writing to beg you home. Little does she guess that you journey still further from her.

WILL My wife! My wife cannot put pen to page, and even if she could, she would not care to. She sends me only complaints and tries for money. No, it is my sister's pages Ned will bring. Be sure to send them to me.

They embrace.

Good fortune, friend.

DICK God speed.

Exit **WILL**.

DICK, *still more dispirited, continues to throw his rings in the vague direction of the stick.*

Enter **HENSLOWE**, *who is much discomfited by the sight of* **DICK**.

HENSLOWE Why must players forever clutter up my theatre? I send them to the mud and filth of the provinces, and lo! the mud and filth remains on my floor.

DICK Calm yourself, Henslowe. You never sent me to the country, and I am clean enough.

HENSLOWE Ah! Dick Burbage. First son of my only rival. Remind me why I don't set my dogs on you.

DICK Because all your dogs were killed for the plague. Leave me be.

HENSLOWE If you will linger in my playhouse, boy, be of some use. The Master of the Revels tells me the daily deaths have dropped. He means to lift the ban. My theatre must be made ready.

DICK Looks ready enough to me.

HENSLOWE *fetches a broom, bucket and cloth.*

HENSLOWE Emptiness breeds dust as the plague breeds pus. Get to it, boy.

DICK I'm not your skivvy.

HENSLOWE Do you want to be a player again? Or would you prefer to go begging back to your father? Your quarrel's no secret, boy.

DICK, *sullen, complies.*

Now. I have a season to open. Where's our ravening young playwright?

DICK Gone.

HENSLOWE Gone?

Trumpets sound. The players are returned.

My boys!

He hurries off. **DICK** *makes to follow him.*

Get to it, Burbage, if you want to eat tonight.

Exit **HENSLOWE**.

Sullen, **DICK** *continues sweeping.*

Enter **JUDITH**, *weary and travel-stained, and in awe of her surroundings.*

JUDITH This is the playhouse. The Rose Theatre –

DICK Theatre's closed.

JUDITH I know. *(In a hushed voice)* Here the stage – there the tiring house – the upper stage – and beyond, the yard, the gallery, and there –

DICK *(hopeful)* Come to clean, have you?

JUDITH *(faintly surprised)* No.

DICK Thought not. You're dressed too fine. Brothel's out back.

JUDITH Oh. No, I'm not – I mean, I'm not here to –

DICK Oh. Beg your pardon.

> **JUDITH** *nods, very cold.*

See, as you're a wench, I thought –

JUDITH Yes. Thank you.

DICK You here to see Joan?

JUDITH Joan?

DICK Henslowe's daughter.

JUDITH *(recognising the name)* Henslowe – yes –

DICK I'll call her. *(Bellows)* Joan! Jo-oan!

> *Enter* **JOAN**, *at a run. She is in the middle of putting up her hair, which tumbles down over her shoulders.*

JOAN Are they here? Has he come?

DICK Joan, there's a wench – ah – a girl here –

NED *(off)* Is that my girl?

> *Enter* **NED**, *at a run.*

JOAN I heard your trumpets.

NED Did they frighten you, little mouse?

> *They kiss, passionately.*

DICK Mistress Henslowe? Joan? Ned?

He is ignored.

JUDITH Oh.

The kiss deepens. Enter **HENSLOWE**.

HENSLOWE Less of that. You're not wedded yet.

NED We're fast betrothed.

HENSLOWE And you'll remain so, boy. Prove yourself worthy of my girl – and all that comes with her.

NED steps back, resentful.

JOAN *(making peace)* Where are the others, Father?

HENSLOWE Unloading my cart. You'll help them.

JOAN and NED start forward. **HENSLOWE** *grabs* **JOAN** *by the shoulder.*

Are your duties done, girl?

She nods. He releases her.

Well, go join them, then.

NED claps DICK on the shoulder as he passes.

NED *(condescending)* Dick.

DICK *(with pride)* Ned.

Exit **NED** *and* **JOAN**.

DICK puts down the broom again.

HENSLOWE Where do you think you're going, boy?

DICK To assist –

HENSLOWE Is my theatre clean? Go to.

Exit **HENSLOWE**.

(off) What have you done with my costumes, you dogs?

A pause.

JUDITH So they are engaged.

DICK These six months.

JUDITH Was that Master Henslowe?

DICK Don't you know that?

JUDITH I'm new to the city.

DICK Come with the players, did you?

JUDITH From Stratford.

DICK Stratford – do you know Master Shakespeare?

JUDITH I do.

DICK Oh! You're here with the message from home?

JUDITH I am the message. Would you be so good as to lead me to him?

DICK You're not his wife, are you?

JUDITH No. His sister. *(Curtseying)* Judith Shakespeare.

DICK *(with a hasty bow)* Dick Burbage at your service. I'm a friend to your brother. But – did his letter not say – did he tell you to meet him here?

JUDITH I thought to surprise him. Could you please convey me to him?

DICK I cannot. I'm so sorry. He's – he's gone.

JUDITH Gone! Do you mean – do you mean he's dead?

DICK No! No, he was well enough, these few hours since. It seems the Earl has found employment for him. Henry Wriothesley, Earl of Southampton.

JUDITH I see.

DICK You've come a long way, on a bad road. You have not been – harmed? The players did not trouble you?

JUDITH Ned ensured that they did not.

DICK Right. *(hollers)* Ned! Ned! Get your arse in here, you pox-scarred whoreson. Ned! What have you done?

JUDITH Master Burbage, please –

Enter **HENSLOWE**, *account book in one hand, quill in another.*

HENSLOWE Take care how you call after my future son-in-law, Master Burbage.

DICK Master Henslowe, wait till you hear – Ned! – he's brought her, Master Henslowe, with her brother gone and no-one to take charge of her – well, he can take her right back again!

HENSLOWE Calm down, Master Burbage, do, and tell me – who is her brother?

JUDITH William Shakespeare is my brother, Master Henslowe. My name is Judith.

JUDITH *curtsies.*

HENSLOWE Delighted. Now, do tell me, Master Burbage – what has my **NED** to do with this?

Enter **NED** *and* **AUGUSTINE PHILLIPS** *(*'**PHIL**'*).*

NED Yes, what has Ned to do with anything? And what in God's name is this frightful row?

Enter **JOAN**.

JOAN Father, three cloaks want darning, and one of the crowns is bent out of shape, and –

HENSLOWE In a minute, my dear. Ned, my boy, it seems that Shakespeare's sister has been brought here under false pretences, and Master Burbage here is of the impression that you are somehow responsible.

PHIL Ned, you old dog –

NED Why, she's here to see her brother! Is he about? Will!

DICK He is not about. He's newly arrived in Titchfield.

NED Well, he must be called back again, at once. Judith has come a long way, at great personal risk –

DICK I'm well aware of that –

JUDITH No. No. He must not be recalled. If he's gone, it's for a reason.

Both **NED** *and* **DICK** *try to reply to this, but* **JUDITH** *ignores them.*

Master Henslowe, I know this is a busy time for you, but might I have your ear for a moment – alone?

HENSLOWE But of course, my dear.

HENSLOWE *draws* **JUDITH** *aside.* **JOAN,** **NED** *and* **PHIL** *busy themselves with the costume trunk, whilst* **DICK** *sweeps around them – all eavesdropping avidly.*

No listening, now, you rogues!

JUDITH I have a proposition for you – a business proposition.

HENSLOWE I'd be happy enough for you to join my girls. But I don't know how I'll face your brother –

JUDITH I mean nothing of the sort, Master Henslowe. Indeed, I do not. My proposition is of quite another kind. I have a play to offer you. I hear you might be in the market.

JUDITH *pulls the pages from the bodice of her dress.*

HENSLOWE A play, indeed? Something new your brother's sent you?

JUDITH It is my own work, Master Henslowe.

HENSLOWE Your own copy?

JUDITH My own words.

She hands the pages to him.

HENSLOWE I see, my dear, I see. What is the title?

JUDITH I call it 'The King's Second Concubine'.

HENSLOWE Speak for me the plot.

JUDITH It is set in ancient Persia –

HENSLOWE Ah! A good location. A love story, is it?

JUDITH Of a sort. The queen disobeys the king, and so is deprived of her position. The King takes as his concubine a young Jewish girl, not knowing her religion.

HENSLOWE There's money in Jews, to be sure – people like to see a villainous Jew.

JUDITH No, no, she is not the villain – for the queen's brother discovers her religion, and persuades the king to condemn all Jews to execution. It is she that saves them –

HENSLOWE Indeed? Rather a forward wench. How does she bring it about?

JUDITH She reveals her identity to save her people. For love of her, the king condemns this former queen and her brother to death, saves the Jewish people, and marries her.

HENSLOWE Very pretty, my dear, though rather hard on the brother. The plot is familiar to me –

JUDITH It is from the Bible. The Book of Esther. But I have focused on what the Biblical tale skirts over – the positions of the two women, the deposed queen and the concubine, as they use the king's favour to battle for their lives. It will make a fit play, I think – in the style of a history, treating tragic matter but ending in marriage and peace.

HENSLOWE Well, you've a knack with words, and clever enough plotting, but I can see you know little of the theatre – as is to be expected from a country girl. It is forbidden, my dear – forbidden to play a Biblical story upon the public stage. Forbidden by the Queen herself, and by the Master of the Revels under her – yes, and by God too, I have no doubt. Put it out of your mind.

JUDITH Then – my play cannot be played?

HENSLOWE Never, my dear.

JUDITH I'll write another. On any subject you name. Oh, it'll take me a small while, Master Henslowe, but I'll write you a play, and a good play, too. I promise you.

HENSLOWE It cannot be done. The Master of the Revels would never allow it – it's no profession for a girl with morals, nor any girl, come to that.

JUDITH I'm far from home, Master Henslowe, and I will not beg, and I will not borrow, and I cannot join the only profession you think open to me. Let me earn my way by my pen, sir, I entreat you.

HENSLOWE And I have a business proposition for you, sweet heart – no, not what you're thinking. A theatre's wealth is in its costumes, and I would hold it a great favour if you would assist me with mine. I'll pay you a fair wage, and you'll work in the theatre – you can watch all the plays and rehearsals if you care to, provided you don't neglect your work and will serve a little ale and fruit on the side. What say you?

JUDITH And if I do all this, will you some day consider what I write?

HENSLOWE Perhaps you may assist your brother. You must take it up with him.

A pause. **JUDITH**'s *dream is in tatters, but she is a stranger in a strange land, and must take what she can get.*

JUDITH I accept your kind offer, Master Henslowe.

HENSLOWE You'll need lodgings, though. Joan will –

JOAN She cannot come in with us, father. The girls are three to a room as it is, and it's hell in working hours –

HENSLOWE Mind your language, Joan. Can she not share with you?

JOAN Father!

HENSLOWE Well, you'll be wedded soon enough, and you've no cause for company there at present –

JUDITH You need not trouble yourself. I will do well enough.

HENSLOWE Just as you like. Well, I've enough to be accounting for – Joan will see to you.

HENSLOWE wanders off, perusing his accounting book, closely followed by **PHIL**.

JOAN *(with unveiled dislike)* Joan will see to you tomorrow. Joan is to the tavern with her betrothed.

NED *(vaguely guilty)* You'll manage well enough, Judith?

JOAN Come, Ned.

NED I'm sorry about your brother.

JUDITH Do not trouble yourself about me, Master Alleyn.

Exit **JOAN** *and* **NED**.

PHIL Master Henslowe, sir, when's our wages due to us? We haven't a coin –

HENSLOWE You've had your allowance.

PHIL Aye, our travel allowance –

Exit **HENSLOWE** *and* **PHIL**, *still bickering*.

(off) – but we're home now!

DICK *continues to sweep.*

DICK You've no lodgings sorted, I suppose?

JUDITH *(near to tears)* I'll manage.

DICK *(sighing)* Come, then. I'll show you to your brother's lodgings. They'll suspect you of being his mistress, mind.

JUDITH That's the least of my worries, now.

DICK Don't take on. You can share my supper – what there is of it. But I must finish this first. And you must send to your brother at first light.

JUDITH You are very kind.

DICK Pure self-interest, I assure you. Here! *(He tosses her a cloth)* You can help.

They set to work. Enter **NED**, *with a flagon of ale.*

NED Judith. Might I beg a word?

JUDITH *(without looking up)* Does your bride-to-be not look for you, Master Alleyn?

NED She can spare me for a moment. A flagon of ale for you, Dick!

DICK And I must drink it outside, I suppose?

NED If you please.

DICK If Master Henslowe sees me, I'll hold you to blame.

NED That's right and fair.

Exit **DICK**, *muttering.*

Judith, please –

JUDITH Does your future bride not await you?

NED You are a lovely girl. I like to flirt with a lovely girl in a country town. Can you blame me if I am not prepared for that lovely girl to follow me back to the city?

JUDITH I did not come to follow you, Master Alleyn.

NED Then where's the harm?

JUDITH You were not honest with me.

NED Honesty can be such a burden to a man... I do not think you are aware of your own loveliness, Judith. Or just how hard it is to resist. Even now, when I look at all that solemn beauty, and those reproachful eyes –

He takes a step towards her, strokes her cheek.

I am sorry for your play, Judith.

Enter **DICK**, *in a temper.* **NED** *steps back, but slowly.*

DICK Now I've Master Henslowe on my back. You may be the pride of the company, Master Alleyn, but it isn't fair to take advantage – I shan't put myself out for you again.

NED Then I'll leave you in peace. One smile before I leave?

JUDITH I hardly think you deserve one.

NED One smile and I will go. You wish me to go, do you not?

JUDITH *(smiling)* You are incorrigible, Master Alleyn.

NED I hope so, Judith.

NED *takes the half-drunk tankard from* **DICK** –

DICK Hey –

– and exits.

You want to watch yourself with that one.

JUDITH I can take care of myself, thank you.

A pause, as **DICK** *cleans, and* **JUDITH** *goes to the trunk and opens it.*

Master Burbage – you are a man of the theatre, are you not?

DICK Born and bred.

JUDITH Then tell me – is it true what Master Henslowe said? Is my play against the law?

DICK What play might that be?

JUDITH Oh come, now. I know you heard me.

DICK Then I think it is. There are those up high that mislike the theatre, and would see us all hanged for traitors. And staging Bible tales has a Catholic smell.

JUDITH I had not thought it was so great a risk.

DICK We must all watch our step in this trade.

> **JUDITH** *is pulling garments from the trunk with interest.*

Enter **PHIL**, *tankard in hand.*

PHIL Dick! When are you joining us?

DICK When I've cleaned this damned place.

PHIL Pshaw! Henslowe's minding our accounts for the road. You've time for a quick one. Besides, we've company –

Exit **PHIL** *for a moment, only to reappear, pulling a giggling* **LUCY MORGAN** *by the hand.*

LUCY My, my. Dick Burbage. I heard you was hanging about the place.

DICK Lovely Lucy Morgan. Where oh where have you been?

LUCY Where's your Master Shakespeare, Dick? I've a hankering to see him.

DICK I thought you were looking for me.

LUCY You don't write me pretty verses.

DICK I'll do you one better. I'll write you a ballad.

He swings around a pillar, and commences singing, loudly and ostentatiously out of tune.

LUCY *(giggling)* No!

DICK *(singing)* Lovely, long-limbed Lucy –

PHIL Dear God!

DICK *(singing)* Her lips are very juicy –

LUCY You never could rhyme, Dick.

DICK *(singing)* She gives her smiles so loosely –

LUCY Charming.

PHIL My ears are bleeding.

DICK And her smiles, they –

He pauses for a moment, at a loss.

JUDITH *(singing in a high, clear voice)* – they seduce me?

PHIL Bravo.

DICK *(singing)* And her smiles, they seduce me! *(to* **JUDITH***)* I thank you.

LUCY *(looking* **JUDITH** *up and down)* And who might you be?

DICK Judith Shakespeare, allow me to present Lucy Morgan, the most famed hussy in the wide world of the theatre.

LUCY You flatter me, Master Burbage – *(noting the name)* Shakespeare?

DICK Well-spotted, Luce, my love. Judith is sister to our very own Will.

LUCY approaches **JUDITH***, who stands still, slightly discomfited, as* **LUCY** *circles her, lifting her hair, stroking her gown, examining her.*

LUCY You look a little like him, you know.

JUDITH Do I?

LUCY Very like. Will you be joining us?

JUDITH I hope so –

DICK Don't misunderstand her, Luce. Shakespeare's sister is not for the likes of you. She's joining the theatre as a seamstress.

LUCY You won't be one of Joan's girls, then?

JUDITH No. Are you?

LUCY I'm the favourite. You do look like him, you know.

> **LUCY** *kisses an astonished* **JUDITH** *on the lips.*

You can give that to your brother for me. Come, Dick.

> *Giggling, she pulls* **DICK** *from the theatre. Exit* **DICK** *and* **LUCY**.

PHIL Join us for a drink, Judith?

JUDITH I've work to do here.

PHIL Come now, don't you mind Henslowe. Nobody does.

JUDITH Well –

PHIL I'm Augustine Philips, mistress, Phil to my friends. I'm known to your brother. Let me treat you to a nip of ale.

JUDITH *(still uncertain)* Thank you.

DICK *(off)* Come along, Phil!

PHIL I'm bringing our guest –

DICK *(off)* Don't trust him Judith, he's got a smooth tongue and a nasty case of the clap!

PHIL Take no notice, mistress. You'll join us in the tavern?

JUDITH I think perhaps I will.

He reaches out his hand, and she takes it. Exit **PHIL** *and* **JUDITH**, *at a run.*

The stage stands empty for moment. A roar can be heard from the tavern next door, and snatches of **DICK**'s *singing.*

Enter **HENSLOWE**, *quill in hand.*

HENSLOWE   Burbage, you useless whoreson! My theatre's not clean yet. Burbage!

Exit **HENSLOWE**, *after the others.*

ACT THREE

Autumn, 1592. The Rose Theatre.

The costume trunk, fully packed and padlocked shut, sits centre stage.

The rest of the stage is bare, but strewn with the debris of a busy season.

NED, half-naked, rests against the trunk. JUDITH, wearing only his shirt, her hair loose about her shoulders, nestles in his arms. Both are half asleep, but struggling to wakefulness.

They cannot let themselves rest.

Birdsong heralds the dawn.

NED kisses JUDITH's head.

NED Almost dawn.

JUDITH *(starting)* I was not asleep.

She makes to kiss him, but he resists.

NED I must dress.

JUDITH Don't go.

NED *(flippant)* Would you have me meet the provinces so? It would shock the more staid of the huswives –

JUDITH No. Don't go. Don't tour.

NED How can I stay? Henslowe orders me.

JUDITH What matters Henslowe? Leave here – leave his daughter. What power has he then?

NED Leave here to go where, Judith? Where would you have me go?

JUDITH Anywhere. Another theatre –

NED Aye, another theatre. Perhaps go to Burbage – he'd have me in a second to spite his son. A new playhouse, with a new stage, but the same scent of ale and dust and crammed, sweating bodies. The rank sweat of the prentices and the perfumed stink of the gentlemen and the rotted nosegays of the whores. Different whores, different players, but the audiences the same. The long succession of afternoons, of rain-soaked plays and sweat-drenched plays and wind that makes my damp skin shiver. Speaking words that are not my own above the roar of the crowd that mocks them. Competing with the bear-baitings where half-crazed animals tear at each other and the crowd screams for their blood, with the hangings where the bodies drop faster than our stage-battles can make 'em. Wet to the skin with stage blood culled from some beast's belly, making a brave death daily as I bruise my shins blue with my fall to the boards. Summers crammed full of plays, full of words, until my head swims with 'em, and my throat is dry and hoarse, and I lose all sense of what I'm speaking. Then the winters, the plague seasons, the numbing tours to God-forsaken towns where none give us welcome – the days without work and without food, scrimping and saving and trying to live. Always the same. Another theatre, but the same.

JUDITH No, Ned. Not the same. With *me*. Another theatre, but with me.

NED Yes, with you, my love. My lovely Judith. Soft and warm beneath the blankets when I return from the playhouse. Your smile on the pillow when I wake. And every morning, your smile would be just a little smaller, in that cramped and dusty room. A little smaller, as the hours lengthen and grow dull while you wait for me, wait through the play you've seen a hundred times before, and the new play so like the old it blurs before you. Smaller, as you wait through the days when I cannot fill the hunger in your belly, as you wait in the icy room I cannot afford to heat. Perhaps a child, a child with your solemn eyes and your tiny cold hands, wailing and screaming because his father cannot keep him warm. Waiting for the court performances that will buy our gifts for Christmas, a Christmas I must miss as I wait on the Queen's command. I touring the provinces, you lonely and jealous in your little room, left behind, dreaming of the family you never see. And finally, old age, and what hope have we then?

JUDITH You are a player. And I have learnt enough these past months to know that is a player's lot, a player's life. It is then so bitter to you?

NED Sometimes.

JUDITH I thought you loved it.

NED I did, once. I'm so tired, Judith. When I think of another year, and another, and another, and the plays never cease —

JUDITH Then you will be so wherever you play. Another theatre will not make you more tired, nor more hungry. What holds you here, Ned? Is it Henslowe? Or his daughter?

NED Henslowe owns this theatre, Judith – aye, and another besides, and half the brothels in the district, and still more. His son-in-law will never hunger, nor will his daughter ever feel cold. Actors are left to rot. They decay with the playwrights in the gutter. Men of business live, and live well. I would live well, Judith. I was not born to starve. And I cannot subject you to such a life —

JUDITH Shall I be safer from starvation because I starve alone? I had a thousand times rather starve at your side. Do not pretend to yourself that you protect me. You do not.

NED I am selfish, Judith. Selfish and a coward. I have not your courage.

A pause.

JUDITH The sun is rising.

NED I must be gone soon.

JUDITH And when you return, you wed, and I may see you no more.

NED Perhaps –

JUDITH No, Ned. No perhaps. Once you return, you shall not see me. I will not make myself an adulteress. I will not damn us both further.

NED Do you think we are damned, Judith?

JUDITH I do not know.

NED Forgive me.

JUDITH Do you love her?

NED Judith –

JUDITH Do you?

NED I have a fondness for her. She is pretty and sharp, has a light step and a ready tongue –

JUDITH She is not a prize mare you are buying!

NED She will be a good wife to me, Judith.

JUDITH And I would not?

NED Oh, my love –

JUDITH Should I be a poor wife to you, Ned? Should I disappoint you?

NED You would be the best of wives, and the sweetest.

JUDITH You do love me, then?

NED Oh, Judith. How could I not? When I see you, my heart stutters in my chest. And when I think that I must leave you, must turn and walk away from you –

JUDITH Oh, my darling!

They reach for one another, almost blindly. As he kisses her lips, face, eyes, neck, he murmurs –

NED I love you, I love you, I love you –

JUDITH I know, I know –

She holds him to her. They kiss again, as if for the last time.

Enter **JOAN**.

JOAN *(softly, almost gently)* I knew it was so.

NED *(leaping up, pulling his clothes about him)* My love!

JOAN To which of us are you speaking, Ned? To your betrothed, or to your whore?

NED Dearest, please –

JUDITH *You* would name *me* a whore?

JOAN Judith Shakespeare, I would brand you the veriest whore that ever took a man between her thighs.

JUDITH And you are such a white-painted angel, Joan Henslowe? Your bed at night lies in a brothel. The dress on your back is paid for with the fruits of whoredom –

JOAN And yours is not?

JUDITH I pay for mine with the work of my hands –

JOAN Your coin comes from the same pot!

NED Girls, please –

JOAN Do not think to order me, Ned! That right was yours when you were to be my husband. You have lost it now.

NED Joan, I beg of you –

JOAN What? What do you beg of me? What can I give you that I have not already given? I have pledged you my body, my wealth, my life. I have given you my heart – you've had that long in your keeping. What more do you want of me, Ned? What more can you ask?

NED Forgiveness.

JOAN Forgiveness! You are only contrite because I have caught you. How many times more would you have lain with her, if I had not spied you?

NED Joan, please – this was the last – this was the final –

JOAN Why limit yourself? Take her all you want. Lie with her till she wears you away, till you're both wasted to the bones. It matters not to me. You matter not to me, Edward Alleyn – I am done with you.

Enter **PHIL**, **LUCY MORGAN** *and* **DOROTHY CLAYTON**.

PHIL What's the yell?

LUCY *(spying* **JUDITH***)* Oh, my.

DOROTHY *begins to laugh.*

PHIL Ned, Ned, Ned. You're an example to us all.

JOAN Get out.

DOROTHY Want me to scratch her, Joan?

NED Joan –

Enter **HENSLOWE**.

HENSLOWE What means this ruckus in my theatre? What is the matter here?

JOAN Papa, I shall never wed.

HENSLOWE Do not speak so rashly, girl. Tell me what…
(catching sight of **JUDITH** *and* **NED***)* Ah. Our playwright's
little sister. I think it best you go to the tiring house
and dress yourself, Judith. Then straightway return.

JUDITH Yes, Master Henslowe.

Exit **JUDITH***, at speed.*

HENSLOWE Master Alleyn. I think it's rather time the
wedding was brought forward, don't you? You've both
been waiting long enough. And a long wait can make a
man restive – is that not so, Ned?

NED Yes – I mean, you are certain – we may still wed?

JOAN I will not wed him, Papa!

HENSLOWE *(aside)* What, would you drive him into her
arms, girl? He's the finest actor this stage has seen.

JOAN And that is all you care for?

HENSLOWE You will wed him, Joan, lest I remember you
are only my step-child, which so far I have contrived to
forget. I care for your future, girl – obey me.

NED Please, Joan – I beg of you –

JOAN No. I will not. I will not.

She begins to sob. He pulls her to him.

Never will I marry you, Ned Alleyn. Never. Never.

NED I am sorry, my love – my little mouse –

JOAN*, still sobbing, relaxes against him.*

JOAN How could you, Ned? How may I trust you now?

NED I'm yours, Joan. I'm yours ever and nobody else's.

Enter **JUDITH***, properly attired but her hair still
dishevelled, carrying* **NED***'s shirt.*

HENSLOWE pulls JOAN away, wipes her tears with his handkerchief.

HENSLOWE *(in a low voice)* You will wed him, then.

JOAN nods.

Good girl.

JUDITH hands the shirt to NED in silence, and he dresses himself in it. All others look away.

NED *(in a low voice)* Farewell, sweet one.

JUDITH *(clearly)* Fare you well, Edward Alleyn.

HENSLOWE Right, my lads. It is time you were on the road. The sun is up!

PHIL and DICK lift and remove the trunk, LUCY and DOROTHY follow. NED and JOAN embrace, and he whispers apologies to her. JUDITH sinks to the ground.

Exit PHIL, DICK, LUCY, DOROTHY and HENSLOWE. NED and JOAN, still embracing, follow.

NED Write me often, my love.

He glances for a moment towards JUDITH, who has her back to him, then exits with JOAN.

JUDITH is alone on the stage, and lets her tears fall. There are trumpets and shouts off.

Enter DICK, calling back over his shoulder.

DICK Bring me back some country ale or a country lass – whichever's the more willing!

He sees the forlorn figure on the floor.

Judith? Are you well?

JUDITH I am quite well.

DICK You shiver.

JUDITH I am cold.

DICK *(making to give her his cloak)* Here –

JUDITH No. It is not a coldness in my skin. It is a coldness *(holding her chest)* here, within my chest, where the wind whistles through.

DICK Ned, then. You miss him already?

JUDITH I miss him now, because he has left me. Tomorrow, he will journey further, and I will miss him more. And when he returns, my longing will grow greater still, because he will be near yet must be apart from me. I know him to be selfish, I know he is not brave, and I know that if he reaches out for me, I must ever after push him away and hate him for it. I know all this, and yet I know that with every day that passes, I will miss him more.

DICK How like your brother you are.

JUDITH My brother?

DICK You could not let Ned be a first love, could you, a short-lived passion, a passing fancy? He could not be a bounder who has hurt you and left you. No, he must be your Love, and though you know his faults, still you will prostrate yourself before his image. You must immortalise your love, so that to forget it breaks your promise to yourself, and to love again becomes a betrayal.

JUDITH Do you speak of me, or of my brother?

DICK I have said too much.

JUDITH What would *he* do, if his love were gone and his hopes vanished?

DICK I'll tell you what he would do, Judith. He would not waste his words on the empty air. He would use his loss. He would write it.

JUDITH Sometimes I fear that there are no words left to me. I have used them all. These months, watching and learning at the theatre, watching in the market places and at the gallows, and I cannot find a single new word, or a new thought. Everything has already been said so much better than I may say it. Every play I watch drives the certainty deeper. I have written all I will ever write. But my tale of a girl who wins the love of a King, who pleads for her people, and saves them, now wears a different face. When I read it, I can only see the tale of a Queen who loses to her rival, who breaks her heart and loses her life. Strange it was that passage Ned chose to read…

DICK When?

JUDITH When we first met.

DICK He read your play?

JUDITH A scene.

DICK And he did not tell you it could never be played?

JUDITH I did not tell him the full story. You cannot always blame Ned, Dick.

DICK Can I not? Look what he has brought you to! An empty theatre and a broken heart.

JUDITH I walked this road myself, Dick. I would not undo the joys I have felt because I have suffered. I would not retrace my steps to Stratford, I cannot wish I'd never seen the Rose or stood upon a stage. I just wish my play could be played – in secret, even, without the knowledge of the authorities – played once, just once, and then my work would not have been wasted. Then I could be at peace.

DICK Judith, to play an unlicensed play will bring imprisonment. To play one that is forbidden can lead only to the Tower.

JUDITH Can the words of a dreaming girl really carry such dark consequences?

DICK They will fear it, Judith.

JUDITH Only if they know of it.

DICK What are you saying?

JUDITH Nothing. Just a thought.

There is a final trumpeting and cheer, off.

DICK Left behind again.

JUDITH Why are you here, Dick? Henslowe offered you a part. My Lord Strange would have you in the company. Why did you remain?

DICK My father's asked me to return.

JUDITH Your father? Dick, that's wonderful! You've made it up?

DICK Not yet. I think we shall. But on one condition – I will not be his. I'm no longer a child. If I returned to him, I'd be my own man. I'd have my own company.

JUDITH Your own?

DICK My father's offered me his theatre – if I'll shake his hand and be friends.

JUDITH So will you do it? Return to your father with your own company of men? Play the lead on your father's stage?

DICK That depends on your brother.

Enter **JOAN**.

JOAN Still here, I see.

JUDITH They are gone?

JOAN And now the time has come for you to leave also.

DICK What? Come now, Joan –

JOAN Hold your tongue, Dick.

JUDITH I did wrong, I know. But I did love him –

JOAN Save your words, and save your sighs. They might have touched Ned's ears, but they do not touch mine. Now go.

DICK Come, do not be so hard, Joan –

JOAN You think to lecture me? Do you even know what has passed? I found them here, still slick with each other's sweat!

DICK You love a player. What else do you expect?

JOAN Would you apply that rule to yourself?

DICK *(bitterly)* Come, I am only a bit part player. You cannot ask me to live up to the standards of our lead.

JOAN And a bit part player you'll remain, unless you learn respect for your betters.

DICK I have no need to curry favour with you, Joan Henslowe. I'll play the lead for my own merits, and not because I've warmed your bed.

JOAN You think your talents are so great, Richard Burbage. But why did they not take you with them? If you are the fine actor you believe yourself to be, why were you left behind?

DICK What do you know of any of it? You stride about this place as if you own it –

JOAN I do –

DICK – and pretend you know the business. But you've never trod these boards for real, never lifted your voice to a crowd – you watch us all, but you've never done it. You know nothing.

JOAN Oh, and you know everything, of course! You players – you're all the same. You waddle and moan and drop upon this stage, and think yourselves so fine. Why a child could do what you do, aye, and do it better, too.

DICK And so could you, I suppose?

JOAN I could out-shout you any day of the week. Out-sob you, out-swoon you, out-screech you. I'd have them weeping in the gallery and howling in the yard.

JUDITH Prove it, then.

JOAN What, Mistress Shakespeare, are you still here?

JUDITH You have every reason to hate me, Joan. But I have a question to ask that you cannot ignore – would you prove it? If you could play a part for real?

DICK *(exasperated)* Judith –

JUDITH I have a play, and there's not a theatre in the city that will take it, because of my sex.

DICK And because it's a forbidden subject –

JUDITH Any subject that I write will be forbidden. No word I write will ever be licensed.

JOAN *(yawning)* Fascinating as I find your sob story –

JUDITH You can never stand upon a stage! No one will pay a single coin to see you play. And why? Because you cannot play at crying? I've seen you turn on the tears many a time when the whorehouse customers cut up rough. Because you cannot be heard? When you raise your voice, half the tavern comes running! Because you wouldn't look well on the stage? Why, you've twice the grace of a skinny boy player, and a woman's face with it. You're barred from the boards, because of your sex. We can neither of us do what we dream of, when the theatres are open and the players are here. Why not join together and make a play in secret, now the players have gone?

DICK I was mistaken, Judith. You're not like your brother. You're far madder than he.

JOAN Oh, hush, Dick.

DICK You're not actually considering it?

JOAN I must think on it.

DICK Of all the damned nonsense –

JOAN I do not mean to like you, Judith Shakespeare. If you wait for my friendship, you will wait long. This changes none of that. But you have a business proposition for me, and I am my father's daughter.

DICK Are you pining for a spell in prison? There are easier ways to make it to the clink.

JOAN I do business with Judith, Burbage. I do none with you.

Enter **LUCY** *and* **DOROTHY**.

LUCY Squabbling again?

DOROTHY She still here, Joan? Want me to kick her for you?

JOAN *(distracted)* Not now, Dot.

DOROTHY Any time, then.

JUDITH There's no need for that.

DOROTHY I'd say there's need enough.

LUCY Let it go, Dot. She's not the first to take another woman's man.

DOROTHY When we do it, we do it honest. Everyone knows what we are. We don't put on airs and graces, with our hair up and paps covered, then go slipping and sliding in dark corners like some back-alley cat.

JUDITH This from the woman in men's attire?

DOROTHY Ah, but you still know I'm a woman, sweetheart, and so does everyone else. I've seen your ways, Judith Shakespeare. Everyone knows what Dorothy Clayton is, and what they'll get from her – be it a kiss or a stabbing. But you – you'd smile in Joan's face one minute, and meddle with Ned the next. I'm sick to the stomach with your coy smiles and your secret glances. Go to, Mistress Shakespeare, if you'd keep your pretty face intact.

DICK That's enough, Clayton –

DOROTHY The day I take orders from you, Burbage, is the day the Thames swallows London. Shakespeare's honey sister is an arrant hobby horse. She's tumbled with Ned enow when our backs were turned, and pranced around the theatre like a little lamb – well it's time she left it.

JOAN Must you, Dorothy?

DOROTHY *(hurt, with bravado)* Et tu, Joanie?

JOAN None of your theatrics. I would *think* for a moment.

LUCY It's so dull now the men are gone. All we do is squabble and fight. And we have to wait the whole winter through till they're back again.

JOAN You need a distraction.

LUCY And where will I find that? I'm as pretty as I can make me, half the students at the Inns are half in love with me, and still there's no chance of an invitation to Easter court. I've waited my whole life to go to court, and soon I'll be old and ugly and I never shall. Even your brother's forgotten me, Judith, though he claimed to love me well enough.

DOROTHY What would you do at Court, my little piece of powdered flesh? They don't send for the likes of us.

LUCY There've been whores in Court masques. I've heard it. They had bare-breasted mermaids once, and there was talk of an Arabian princess. I could play in their little interludes as well as any.

JOAN *(deciding)* Would you be a player if you could, Lucy?

LUCY Would I? I'd better the player boys any day.

JOAN Judith here has a little scheme. She'd have us in a secret play. Are you with us, Luce? A part with lines and love and death is better than a silent mermaid.

LUCY But it's against the law.

JOAN You silly goose, all we do here is against the law. Why should this be any different? *(To* **JUDITH***)* I'll play the queen.

JUDITH Of course.

LUCY Why should Joan always have her way? I would be the queen.

JUDITH Joan shall play Vashti, the queen who is deposed. You shall play Esther, the concubine who becomes queen.

LUCY I become queen?

DICK How many women's parts are there to this play?

JUDITH Four. The queen, the concubine, two handmaids.

DICK And how many parts in total? How many?

JUDITH Nine.

DICK And who will play the rest?

JOAN Why, my girls, of course.

DICK Women play as men? No one will believe it. You will be as laughing stocks.

DOROTHY You shall not stop me playing the villain, Master Dick, for all your stern looks. I've watched Ned Alleyn boom and thunder on the stage enough. I can do it as well. I've always hankered to play the villain. There is a villain?

JUDITH There is. Haman, the queen's brother.

DOROTHY Then him I will play.

DICK A man!

DOROTHY Yes, a man! Why should I not? I've worn men's attire half my life. Why should I not do it on the boards?

JOAN Men play as women. Why is this strange?

DICK It will be foolish! The villain can be played as a woman, yes. And perhaps the guards, or the old uncle. But what of the king?

JOAN What of him?

DICK Show me one of your girls who can carry off the king.

LUCY What does it matter? No one will see us play it. It's just for the fun of it.

JOAN No. No, I will not risk a whipping and my father's displeasure for a moment's amusement. I will not play a joke. If we do this, we do it well.

JUDITH But she's right, Joan. We have to perform it in secret. If the authorities find us – we're lost.

JOAN Do you think whoring is legal in this city? Our customers know how to keep a secret. So do all the girls of this trade. We cannot invite the tradesmen and their wives, the respectable folk who gossip and let their tongues wag free. But the keepers of secrets, those who know how to hold their tongues and move in the shadows, those who live in the dark like us – they can come without harming us, and I will tell them so.

DICK I would not advise it –

JUDITH Play with us. Play the king. You always claim to be a man of the theatre, Dick. You say it's in your blood and your bones. You say your talent's hidden by other men, you say your father chokes it and Ned Alleyn obscures it – if this is so, then show us.

DICK Do you know what you're asking me, Judith? I am a real player, a professional. And you ask me to act in an illicit play, in a stolen theatre, with a gaggle of girls?

JUDITH Yes.

DICK I think not.

JUDITH Then we'll do it without you.

DICK I'll tell.

JUDITH You wouldn't –

JOAN If my father discovers us, we are all of us on the streets.

DICK Better destitute than dead.

JOAN You'll not ruin me, Dick Burbage. I'll not stand by to see it.

JUDITH Join us, Dick.

DOROTHY He won't.

DICK You're damn right I won't.

JUDITH Why?

DOROTHY Because he's a coward. A lily-livered coward.

DICK If you were a man, *Mistress* Clayton, I'd stab you for that.

JUDITH Play with us, Dick. Show us you can play the king.

DICK I have no need to prove myself to you.

JUDITH Nor to yourself?

Lights down.

ACT FOUR

HENSLOWE*'s brothel, 'The Little Rose'.*

JOAN, LUCY, DOROTHY *and* DICK *are rehearsing, while* JUDITH *writes.*

LUCY What's that?

DOROTHY It's just passers-by, Luce.

LUCY I thought I heard drums.

DOROTHY No drums, my dear. Not yet.

DICK What's up with you, Lucy? You're as skittish as an untrained mare.

LUCY It's Shrove Tuesday. Today's the day they come for us.

DOROTHY Now, now, Luce my girl –

LUCY I saw them. Last year. I watched them. I hid in rags in a gutter, and I saw them drag the girls from the brothels, pull them by their hair. They ripped the clothes from their bodies and dragged them behind carts. Their scalps were bleeding by the time they were done, and their skin all over bruises and their legs and shoulders scratched and raw. I don't want them to take me.

DICK We can't stop for a day, Lucy. This is the only day in the calendar we can be sure you girls won't be called off for your – er – other duties. The players will return before the end of Lent, and then we're finished.

LUCY But what if they come for us? They'll ruin my face. I can't play a queen with a bleeding face. How will I ever be seen at Court if they scar me?

DOROTHY There, there, love. It's not so bad. They took me last year, and I survived it well enough. Sometimes they let you ride on the cart – they bare your breasts and display you through the streets! It's like a parade.

JOAN They will not come here. My father's bribed half the soldiers in the district, and he has many friends. They will not trouble us.

DICK   There, girls. Henslowe wouldn't leave you unprotected. Besides, I'm here.

DOROTHY Fat lot of good you'd do us. There's not an ounce of muscle on you!

JOAN You could always fence them –

DOROTHY I hear stage swords are ever so frightening –

JOAN Grown soldiers faint when they see them –

LUCY And then you could roar at them!

JOAN With your angry glare –

DOROTHY They'd back out in a trice –

DICK Alright, alright, girls. Leave a man with a shred of dignity.

The girls continue to laugh.

Don't you have rehearsing to do?

JUDITH *sits at the side, trying to write.*

Her fingers are inky and stained, and there is a smudge of ink upon her cheek.

DICK *goes to sit by her.*

How goes it?

JUDITH Ill. I cannot seem to write the end. And we must rehearse it tomorrow, if we are to be ready within the week.

DICK Well, tell me where you are.

JUDITH I just cannot decide if it should end happily.

DICK For the deposed queen?

JUDITH Oh, no. For Esther. It cannot end happily for the queen. Queen Vashti must die.

DICK Why must she?

JUDITH *(turning to him properly)* Because she cannot have what she wants. The king and Esther love one another. They have a hope, a future. But the queen has nothing. She is born into the wrong time, and there is nothing she can do to change it.

DICK Don't move.

JUDITH What is it?

  DICK *licks his thumb and rubs at her cheek.*

DICK Ink.

  They stare at one another.

  Judith –

  Banging at the door.

  LUCY *shrieks.* **DOROTHY** *pulls out a knife.*

JUDITH What –

DICK It's only –

JOAN Hush. Hide.

  The other girls back into corners, as **JOAN** *goes to the door.*

DICK You needn't –

JOAN *holds her fingers to her lips.*

JOAN Who is it?

PHIL *(off)* Let me in.

JOAN We don't admit strangers here. Who knocks?

PHIL *(off)* Don't you know me, Joan? It's Phil –

JOAN *flings open the door.*

JOAN Phil! You scared us half to death.

DOROTHY Shame on you, man. Don't you know it's Shrove Tuesday?

LUCY *throws herself at him.*

LUCY We thought you was in the provinces!

PHIL I was called back.

JOAN Who by?

DICK Have you brought them?

PHIL Ay. A tonne weight.

Enter **PHIL**, *dragging a trunk.*

DICK I'll stand you a pint of ale for this.

PHIL I near broke my back. For this, I'll take a pint of canary.

DICK Done.

JOAN You knew?

DICK I ordered these costumes, woman. Of course I knew.

JOAN You knew he was at the door. While we were shaking in our boots. And not a word –

DICK You silenced me!

JOAN My patience is wearing thin, Master Burbage. Take care it doesn't snap.

LUCY *(opening the trunk)* Look.

DOROTHY *(pulling out a stage sword)* This'll do me.

JOAN This is your father's hoard. It must be worth a fortune.

DICK It is.

JOAN *(pulling out costumes)* Dick – thank you.

DICK Perhaps I may trespass upon your patience a little longer?

PHIL I'd best be off.

JOAN So soon?

LUCY Stay, Phil. Stay and watch us.

PHIL I wish I could. But I'm ordered to –

He pauses.

DICK Double-dealing again, my friend? Well, I wish you luck with your secrets.

PHIL Thanks, Dick. I – yes. Goodbye.

LUCY Aren't you going to wish us luck, Phil?

Exit **PHIL**.

That was rude.

DOROTHY What's he up to?

LUCY Why wouldn't he wish us luck?

DICK Don't bother your little head about him. He's always off on crooked business. Now, are we to have a rehearsal, or no?

LUCY But –

JOAN Peace, Lucy. The confrontation scene. We'll do that.

They don their costumes, and step into place.

JOAN I am come to beg for my brother, my lord.

DICK He is to die. Now leave me.

She kneels to kiss his feet, a shower of passionate kisses.

JUDITH *stops scribbling, and begins to watch, growing gradually more agitated.*

JOAN Is there nothing I can do?

He stands and walks from her. She grasps his hand to kiss it, but he pulls it from her.

DICK I have already signed the papers for his execution. You can do nothing.

She makes to kiss his neck, and again he pushes her from him.

JOAN My kisses were not always so distasteful to you.

DICK Vashti, I shudder at your kisses. They are the cold, empty kisses of a corpse. You are dead to me.

JOAN *pulls out a knife from where it sits against her thigh.*

DICK *flinches back but* **JOAN**, *laughing, holds the knife against her own throat.* **DICK** *approaches her, but* **JOAN** *backs off, still tracing the knife against her skin.*

JOAN You were angry with me. I disobeyed you. I could have lanced your anger as one lances a boil, bled it dry. I could have sucked it from you with one of my kisses. But you would not see me.

JUDITH No – no, that's wrong. Like you're quarrelling.

JOAN *(with resentment)* But we are quarrelling.

JUDITH Stage quarrelling. It isn't supposed to be real. It belongs to the world of the play, where everything is bigger, brighter, more beautiful. It should be declaimed.

DICK Like the great Ned Alleyn, you mean.

JUDITH Yes. Exactly.

DICK Why?

JUDITH Because I wrote it so. I dreamt those words. I know how they should sound.

DICK I see. And when you wrote them, had you ever loved?

JUDITH Of course –

DICK As a woman loves a man?

JUDITH Not as such, but –

DICK Had you ever had your heart broken?

JUDITH No.

DICK Had you ever suffered as she has suffered?

JUDITH No.

DICK And have you now? Do you know now how a broken heart feels?

JUDITH *(very soft)* Yes.

DICK How does it feel? Is it a declamation? Is it a cry and a roar and a thundering?

JUDITH No. It's an ache. A veil drawn over colours and shapes and sounds that were sharp and bright and clean. It's a dullness, a pain, a weight in your chest.

DICK *(to* **JOAN**) Show us.

> **JOAN** *continues the scene from those last lines, but this time, she is not only passionate, but vulnerable, and we warm to her.*

JOAN You were angry with me. I disobeyed you. I could have lanced your anger as one lances a boil, bled it dry. I could have sucked it from you with one of my kisses. But you would not see me.

DICK Cease this, Vashti.

JOAN Spare my brother.

DICK No.

JOAN You feared me. You feared my power over you. When I disobeyed you, you feared the whole kingdom would know of my power. The whole world.

DICK Enough.

JOAN Spare my brother.

DICK No.

> **JUDITH**, *inspired, scribbles the final line of the play, then puts it aside to watch.*

JOAN You could not see me, because you feared these chains still held you. They still do. This hair – you have lain on it, cried into it, twined your fingers around it. You have kissed every inch of this skin. This womb – this barren, empty womb that will ever be empty, that shall have worms crawl and burrow and breed in it – this womb has carried your babes and you have whispered to them within it. This body, this body you took and used and loved, this body bound you to me, and so you had it locked away.

DICK Vashti, cease!

JOAN Spare my brother!

DICK No.

JOAN Then kill me.

> *A trumpeting sounds out, accompanied by the banging of drums, and the clattering of boots. All freeze.* **LUCY** *runs to the window, draws back the shutters, looks out.*

LUCY It's the soldiers. They are coming. They are coming for us.

> *A moment of frozen terror, and then all move.*

DOROTHY We'll tell them this is not a brothel. We'll tell them it's a theatre property, that this is a rehearsal –

DICK With women? With women players?

JOAN Women players, and an unlicensed play. They'll make an example of us. They'll lock us away –

JUDITH This is not just an unlicensed play. It's a forbidden play. If they find it, we're for the Tower.

DICK If they find it, we are dead.

JUDITH Give me the pages. I'll burn them.

Banging at the door.

DICK Too late!

Banging again.

JUDITH *snatches up all the pages, and disappears.*

DICK *removes his costume, and then most of his clothes, at speed.*

JOAN What in God's name are you doing?

DICK Look like whores.

DOROTHY Have you gone mad? We *are* whores.

Banging again.

DICK Just look like it! This is a brothel, understood? And you are all whores. And that is all that's happening here. If we're lucky, they'll whip you, and leave it at that.

LUCY Whip us? They'll do worse. They'll drag us by our hair. Parade us through the streets. Pull us behind horse-drawn carts. They'll strip us!

DICK And you'll live. It's this or death.

Banging, even louder.

FIRST SOLDIER Open up, or I break the door down!

> **DICK** *grabs* **DOROTHY**'s *fencing sword, and covers his face with a mask.*

That's it! One, two –

> **DICK** *throws open the door.*

DICK Enter at your peril.

> *Enter* **SERGEANT** *and* **TWO SOLDIERS**.

SERGEANT Put that down. Put it down! Your stage silver won't help you. *(Looking about him)* Ah. Better than I'd hoped. A nest of whores and vipers.

> **FIRST SOLDIER** *grabs at* **DICK**, *and pulls the mask from his face.*

Ah! Richard Burbage. Just the other day, your father assured me that he was an upstanding businessman.

DICK My father has no part in this.

SERGEANT I doubt that. There's half his costumes in here. *(he spots* **DOROTHY***)* Whores in boys' clothes? Do we have ourselves a company of players?

DICK Don't be ridiculous, man. They're women!

SERGEANT Then why is this one dressed as a man? And this one as a queen? And this one – hello, sweetheart – as some sort of exotic strumpet?

LUCY I'm a concubine, actually.

JOAN Lucy!

SERGEANT Explain that if you can, Master Burbage. Why exactly are these girls wearing the Theatre's wardrobe?

DICK I should have thought that was obvious. They are whores. I am their customer.

SERGEANT *(looking at the assembled women)* The only customer?

DICK Yes.

SERGEANT *(to* **SECOND SOLDIER***)* Look around.

   Exit **SECOND SOLDIER**.

DICK I – er – happen to have an inclination towards women in men's clothes.

SERGEANT And in women's clothes.

DICK Yes, and in women's clothes.

SERGEANT And – royalty?

DICK A man can dream, officer.

   FIRST SOLDIER *snickers.*

SERGEANT Your father may be less than happy with how you choose to spend his savings, Master Burbage. But you admit that these are whores?

DICK I do indeed.

SERGEANT And that this is a whorehouse?

   DICK, *realising the trap into which he has fallen, is silent.*

   JOAN *steps forward.*

JOAN Gentlemen, what is it that you want? Are you looking to avail yourself of our services? Because there are rather a number of you, and, as you can see, we are occupied at present –

SERGEANT You are aware, madam, that whoring is illegal? *(to* **SOLDIER***)* We'll take the girls first.

JOAN You shall not drag me behind that cart.

SERGEANT You're right about that.

   He grabs her, and rips the top of her dress from her, exposing her slip.

We'll do you one better. You'll ride high on the cart, for all to see!

DICK *(brandishing his sword again)* Touch them at your peril.

They grab his sword from him and push him back.

JOAN My father shall hear of this.

SERGEANT We'll get your father next, girl.

Exit **FIRST SOLDIER**, *with* **JOAN**.

DICK This is ridiculous. I demand that you unhand me.

SERGEANT Then let us do our duty, Master Burbage, and you can go free – this time.

DICK You think I'd stand back and let –

SERGEANT I think you'll allow us to treat these whores however we please – or I might become curious as to where these costumes come from.

DICK *slouches back, beaten.*

Enter **FIRST SOLDIER**.

LUCY Don't let them take me!

DOROTHY *(blocking* **LUCY***)* Touch her and I'll cut you.

SERGEANT You're only making it worse for yourself, Mistress Clayton.

A shriek is heard off-stage.

Enter **JUDITH**, *pulled by* **SECOND SOLDIER**, *who holds her pages in his hand.*

SECOND SOLDIER She was trying to burn them, Sarge.

JUDITH Can't I use old papers for kindling?

SERGEANT Rather a warm day to light a fire in an empty room. What's your name, girl?

JUDITH Judith Shakespeare.

SERGEANT Shakespeare, is it? Any relation?

JUDITH To whom?

SERGEANT I'm not a simpleton, madam. I've had many – dealings – with the players and their kind. Are you related to William Shakespeare, playwright, actor, and vagabond?

JUDITH William Shakespeare is my brother, and he is no vagabond.

SERGEANT They're all the same to me, sweetheart. Now, why did your brother give you this play?

JUDITH He didn't.

SERGEANT Then how did you come to possess it?

JUDITH I wrote it.

> **SERGEANT** *and* **SOLDIERS** *laugh.*

SECOND SOLDIER We've a feisty one here.

SERGEANT Take the girls out, lads. I'll deal with this.

> **SECOND SOLDIER** *grabs* **LUCY**, *while* **FIRST SOLDIER** *reaches for* **DOROTHY**, *who goes for him with her knife but is quickly disarmed. Exeunt, whilst* **SERGEANT** *peruses the pages.*

DICK She's lying. It's not hers.

JUDITH Don't bother, Dick.

DICK She's just pretending – she's – she's mad –

SERGEANT Stow it a minute, Master Burbage. What is this, mistress?

JUDITH A play.

SERGEANT Yes, I can see that. But what is it?

JUDITH The King's Second Concubine.

SERGEANT And what is the plot?

JUDITH Esther, a young Jewish girl, marries the King and saves her people.

SERGEANT Esther from the Book of Esther? A Bible play? Your brother dared write this?

JUDITH He did not.

SERGEANT Your defence won't last long, mistress. This is out of my hands. I'll have to take you to the Tower – and the men there'll make you speak quickly enough.

DICK No. I wrote it. Take me to the Tower, but leave her.

JUDITH He didn't! He's lying. He just wants to protect me –

SERGEANT How does it end?

DICK I cannot recall.

SERGEANT Nonsense. The page is uppermost. The ink is still wet. What's the final line?

> DICK *struggles, then hangs his head.*

Tell us, girl. Whose is this?

JUDITH It's mine.

SERGEANT And who wrote it, fool?

JUDITH I did.

He strikes her.

DICK No!

> DICK *starts forward, but he is dragged back.*

SERGEANT Who wrote it?

JUDITH I did.

He strikes her again, harder.

SERGEANT Now. Answer me. Was it your brother?

JUDITH No.

He strikes her again.

SERGEANT Take her.

DICK Judith.

JUDITH Dick –

He grasps her hand. Their eyes meet for a moment, and it means something. But then she is dragged away.

DICK Judith!

Exit the **SERGEANT** *and* **FIRST SOLDIER**, *with* **JUDITH**.

I'll get her back! Do you hear me? You will live to regret this! I have many friends –

DICK *sinks to the ground, his head in his hands.*

Enter **WILL**, *weary, travel-stained and sad.*

WILL What in the name of God has happened here?

DICK *stares at him.*

Blackout.

ACT FIVE

A cell in the Tower of London.

JUDITH, *her leg bound in iron, sits upon the floor. Her cell is small and sparse. It is very dark. Moonlight through the window is the only illumination.*

JUDITH *is praying softly, under her breath. She has been speaking the same words for some time, keeping despair at bay.*

JUDITH Thy kingdom come; thy will be done, in earth as it is in heaven. Give us this day our daily bread, and forgive us our trespasses, as we forgive them that trespass against us. And lead us not into temptation; but deliver us from evil.

Enter **JAILOR**, *carrying a lantern, with* **THOMAS EGERTON**, *the Queen's Attorney General. He is practised in the interrogation and prosecution of Catholics, spies and traitors, but he is uneasy – he is unused to interrogating young women.*

JAILOR *unlocks* **JUDITH**'s *door.*

EGERTON Thank you, Hardshaw. I'll take those.

JAILOR hands EGERTON the keys, places the lantern upon the ground and exits.

Good evening. My name is Egerton. I am Attorney General of the realm and I am here at Her Majesty's bidding. I am here to discuss this play that you claim is yours.

JUDITH It is mine.

> EGERTON *sits upon the stool, and gestures to the bed.*
> JUDITH *rises, with difficulty, and sits herself upon it.*

EGERTON You are in a difficult and dangerous situation here. Utter and complete honesty is all I can advise.

JUDITH I will speak the truth, sir, but I will not speak that which may bring trouble upon my friends. You cannot expect me to harm them.

EGERTON Not to do so will bring greater trouble upon yourself. I advise you to be frank. Speak for me your name.

JUDITH Judith Shakespeare.

EGERTON And your station in life?

JUDITH The daughter of John Shakespeare, of Stratford.

EGERTON And your brother?

JUDITH My brother is William Shakespeare.

EGERTON What is his position?

JUDITH He is a playwright.

EGERTON For which company?

JUDITH My Lord Strange's Men, of late.

EGERTON And where does he reside at present?

JUDITH I have heard rumours. I have no certain knowledge –

EGERTON Then tell me what you suspect.

JUDITH I believe he resides with his patron.

EGERTON And his patron is…?

JUDITH Henry Wriothesley, the Earl of Southampton.

> EGERTON *is visibly surprised.*

EGERTON If this be so, then it is the worse for you. And how did you come to be in London?

JUDITH I travelled with the players, to sell my play.

EGERTON To whom?

JUDITH Philip Henslowe.

EGERTON Did he accept it?

JUDITH No.

EGERTON For what reason?

JUDITH My sex.

EGERTON And was that the only reason?

JUDITH Yes.

EGERTON Your sex was the only reason Master Henslowe declined to buy this play?

JUDITH *(more hesitantly)* Yes.

EGERTON You are willing to swear that?

JUDITH I – yes.

EGERTON In the name of the Queen?

> *Pause.*

> Will you swear in the Queen's name, with a hand on the Word of our Lord?

JUDITH No.

EGERTON There was another reason that Henslowe would not touch your play?

JUDITH It is a Biblical play.

EGERTON And why did this convince Henslowe not to take it?

JUDITH Because it is forbidden.

EGERTON For what reason?

JUDITH I do not know.

EGERTON Then I will inform you. It is forbidden because the staging of Biblical history may encourage irreverence, and it may encourage idolatry.

JUDITH But my play is neither irreverent nor idolatrous.

EGERTON That is not for you to decide.

JUDITH Have you read my play?

EGERTON I have read it.

JUDITH Did you think it idolatrous? Did you think it irreverent?

EGERTON It is right that you admire your brother's work. You cannot be expected to comprehend what it might mean.

JUDITH Why do you persist in referring to the play as my brother's work?

EGERTON Why do you persist in the fiction that it is yours?

JUDITH It is mine. I do not know how to prove it to you. The hand is mine, but you will say I have copied it. I know the lines by heart, but you will say I have conned them. The plot itself is history, but each alteration is mine, every line of speech is mine, every character is mine. I dreamt them up. Show me a way to prove this to you, and I will do so.

EGERTON I do not pretend to accept that you wrote this play. But I must warn you that if you persist in these lies, they will mean your death.

JUDITH And if I break my word, and pretend I did not write it, it will mean the death of my brother.

EGERTON You admit, then, that you are lying to protect your brother?

JUDITH No. I am speaking the truth to protect my brother.

EGERTON I am striving to make you understand. There is a playwright languishing in the next cell but one, subject to daily torture to wrench confession for atheism from him. Another, a spy and perhaps a traitor, is under house arrest in the city, as the net is drawn ever closer about him. But each has been watched for months, and neither had a hand in this play. Your brother has held himself apart and walks free, and now his sister is discovered in a brothel with a fatal play about her person. I would have him dead for the writing of it and yourself in the Clink for attempting to purvey it. But if your brother is under the protection of the Earl of Southampton, then unless we can prove the play is his, we may not touch him. Someone must burn for this. Take care it is not you.

JUDITH Should not the author of the work take responsibility for it?

EGERTON You will protect your brother and damn yourself!

JUDITH I will not be damned. I tell you now, as I shall tell my Lord and Saviour when I stand before him on the Day of Judgement – I wrote this play.

EGERTON And you see nothing in this play to damn you Judith? Nothing to concern the Master of the Revels? Nothing the Queen may mislike?

JUDITH Nothing.

EGERTON Your play tells of an ageing and childless queen, a queen whose throne is usurped because she will not be subject to the rule of men. This queen is usurped by a young, beautiful, fertile girl, a girl who follows in secret a foreign and maligned religion. This girl's marriage protects all those who are persecuted because of this religion, and ensures the death of the queen and her advisers. Can you truly not see how this may be read as treason?

JUDITH I had not seen it so before. I swear to you, I had not. It is a Bible tale; I was true to the version in the

Geneva Bible. How can the Word of our Lord be treason?

EGERTON There are those who would see treason in it, Mistress Shakespeare. There are those who would be glad to. I was a Catholic myself, once, before I saw the error of my ways. Had I read your play then, I should have seen a secret message in it. And because I have strayed near treachery myself, I know innocence when it sits before me. You cannot read the secrets of this play, and so I ask you again – where did you procure it?

JUDITH I did not procure it. I wrote it.

EGERTON Did your brother send it to you?

JUDITH No.

EGERTON Was it given to you by another playwright?

JUDITH No.

EGERTON You speak in the sight of God, and at the command of your Queen, Judith.

JUDITH I know it, Master Egerton.

Enter **PHIL***, a cloaked and hooded figure. He bows, ignoring* **JUDITH***.*

PHIL Sir Thomas –

EGERTON There's no need to 'Sir' me, man. I haven't been knighted yet.

PHIL If the rumours are correct, Sir, you will not have long to wait.

EGERTON You've a keen ear for rumours.

PHIL It's what you pay me for, Sir.

JUDITH I know your voice.

PHIL I doubt it.

EGERTON You don't want her to know you, then?

JUDITH What are you? A spy?

EGERTON He has spied upon you, Judith, and upon those nearest to you.

PHIL Sir!

EGERTON It's true enough. You're the Queen's man through and through.

JUDITH I count myself the Queen's woman, Master Egerton, but I cannot see why she must spy upon her loyal subjects.

PHIL This innocence of yours can become wearing, Judith. Isn't now the time to drop it?

> **PHIL** *drops his hood.*

I am a loyal man, Judith, but my Queen must come first –

EGERTON Your Queen and a good deal of coin, man. Let's not give ourselves airs.

JUDITH How could you? You – how could you?

PHIL You have no conception of how hard it can be. Pretty Judith Shakespeare, with your sweet smile and your beguiling ways, with your false piety and your little Bible play, with half the players in love with you and even the whores protecting you – what do you know of suffering? What do you know of hunger and debt? I told your crimes to the crown. A man must live.

JUDITH You sold us.

PHIL I did not betray innocents. You each of you had something to hide.

JUDITH But – they were your friends, Phil. They dragged them through the streets – Dot, Joan, little Lucy – we were your friends. I was your friend.

PHIL May I report to you now, Sir?

EGERTON Do so, Phillips, and quickly.

PHIL May I not speak to you in – ah – in private?

EGERTON What you have to say concerns Mistress Shakespeare nearly.

PHIL I know it, Sir. That's why I'd speak to you alone.

EGERTON Spit it out, man.

PHIL William Shakespeare did not write that play.

EGERTON And you can prove that, can you? You have his word?

PHIL Not his word alone. The word of the Earl of Southampton. He says the playwright has been in his company these six months.

EGERTON That is no proof –

PHIL He swears it, Sir. The Earl swears on Will's innocence. Would you challenge his word?

EGERTON Then the blame must fall on Judith alone? This unschooled chit of a girl with no more cunning than an unweaned lamb?

PHIL I'm sorry for it, Judith.

JUDITH Save your breath.

EGERTON Leave us.

PHIL Sir.

Exit **PHIL**.

EGERTON I would help you, girl.

JUDITH I thank you, sir. But you cannot. It is my writing, and I cannot escape that.

EGERTON Then there may be nothing more that I can do for you. You swear in the name of the Queen and on the word of our Lord that you, Judith Shakespeare, are the sole author of this seditious and treasonous play?

JUDITH It is not seditious and treasonous. I will not swear to that.

EGERTON But you swear this is your play?

JUDITH I, Judith Shakespeare, swear in the name of the Queen and on the Word of our Lord that I am the sole author of The King's Second Concubine, and that I did come to London to sell it to a playing company and see it performed. My brother has no knowledge of this play. I take sole and absolute responsibility for it. If The King's Second Concubine is in any way immoral, idolatrous, irreverent, seditious, or treasonous, then on my head be it.

EGERTON Then God rest your soul, Judith Shakespeare, for I cannot save you.

> **EGERTON** *blows out the lantern. There is only moonlight. Exit* **EGERTON***.*

> *A long pause, when all that can be heard is* **JUDITH**'s *sobbing, which gradually peters out. Then, a knocking.*

WILL *(off)* Show me to Judith Shakespeare.

JAILOR *(off)* I dare not, sir.

WILL You saw the carriage that brought me here, did you not? Did you mark the coat of arms?

JAILOR Yes, sir.

WILL Then admit me, man.

> *Enter* **WILL***.*

Judith?

JUDITH *(in a piercing whisper)* Will!

WILL Judith –

JUDITH Oh, Will –

WILL Little one. How in God's name have you ended in such a place as this?

JUDITH I followed you, Will. I followed my dream.

WILL Oh, Judith. Why?

JUDITH Why did you come to London?

WILL That is not an answer. We are not the same.

JUDITH Are we not?

WILL You know we are not. I could earn my living by my pen, live alone without a scandal, leave my family with a good name, and prosper. You could not.

JUDITH No. I did better. I do not leave a family behind in Stratford, and live alone at their expense. I refused a loveless marriage.

WILL And ruined yourself, Judith.

JUDITH Come, Will – must we speak of this now? This may be the last time –

WILL Don't, Judith. I cannot bear it.

JUDITH You must. If I can bear it, you can. Now quickly, before our time runs out – are you happy?

WILL What a question, for such a time –

JUDITH With the Earl. Does he make you happy? Does the poetry make you happy?

WILL It would be any poet's dream –

JUDITH But you are not only a poet, Will. Once you were a playmaker.

WILL There are no gentleman playmakers. Our father's request for a coat of arms was never granted. I would make our family great.

JUDITH Who reads your work as a poet?

WILL The Earl, his friends – the finest men of the realm.

JUDITH You are wasting your talents on a tiny circle? Dribbling your words out for a pampered few who do not need them?

WILL I have plans to publish – but that is not what I came for, Judith. Why do you speak of this now?

JUDITH Because I have almost no time left. I cannot write the plays I dreamed of. Plays not for the few, but for the many. I cannot even see my play performed.

WILL Judith, Dick asked me to tell you –

JUDITH Yes?

WILL He asked me to say that they will play your play. In Dick's father's theatre, in secret, before the players return. They will play it to whoever will come, and damn the consequences. Your work will not die with you.

JUDITH The girls are well, then?

WILL They live.

JUDITH Thank Dick for me. Thank them all.

WILL Is it worth it then? Is your play worth dying for?

JUDITH How can you ask me that?

WILL Judith, I was ever a cautious man. I take every care. I pander to those in power and will not risk my neck for a cause or a dream. Fellow pensmen die in the gutters, and I do not take a step to save them. My one dream is to die a prosperous and contented gentleman, with my genius acknowledged and work that will live beyond me. But I would not die for it.

JUDITH Perhaps it is easier for me to die as a writer. I have no chance of living as one.

WILL Did you never hope for a woman's lot? A husband, children, home and hearth?

JUDITH Perhaps I did once, Will. Perhaps I once hoped for a Stratford lad who would love me. I dreamed of strolling with him in fields of corn, and kissing him in the woods in May when all the town ran riot. I dreamed of marriage in the whitewashed church where I was baptised, and churching my own children there. I dreamed of a family around me and a life filled with love. But I chose something else.

JAILOR Master Shakespeare. It will be dawn soon. You must be gone.

WILL It cannot be so soon!

A cockerel crows.

But half an hour longer.

JAILOR There is not time.

WILL I love you, Judith. You have written a fine play, and I am well proud of you, chuck.

JUDITH Promise me something, Will.

WILL Anything.

JUDITH Promise to write a play. Just one more. Return to the theatre, Will. Return to your friends. Promise me.

WILL I must go grovelling back to Henslowe? Live under his yoke again?

JUDITH No, Will. Dick is forming a company. Let your words be heard.

The bells chime out.

JAILOR Away.

WILL But while we say one prayer!

JAILOR Be gone!

JUDITH Promise me, Will.

WILL I promise. Little one –

JUDITH Will, I'm scared.

WILL I'll be there.

JUDITH No –

WILL I will –

JUDITH Don't watch it. Watch my play.

WILL Judith –

JUDITH Remember your promise. Remember me!

Exit **WILL** *with* **JAILOR**, *who pulls him from the stage.*

Remember me.

JUDITH *is very still for a moment. Then she kneels and crosses herself.*

Blackout.

Curtain.

PROPERTY LIST

ACT ONE

Judith's play

Inkpot filled with ink

Quill

Handkerchief

A floorboard that can be lifted to hide/reveal play and inkpot

Shawl

Pheasants

Will's letter to Judith

'Fire'/illusory fire in the fireplace

Pitcher of water

Pot of stew and spoon

ACT TWO

Dick's wooden rings and stick

Dick's broom, bucket and cloth

Henslowe's account book and quill

Ned's flagon of ale

Costume trunk, containing theatre costumes

ACT THREE

Bed sheet for Ned and Judith

Dorothy's knife

ACT FOUR

Actors' "parts" (sheets of paper with lines and three-word cues) for *The King's Second Concubine*

Stage sword, mask, crowns for a king and queen and a costume for a concubine (which must all fit in the trunk)

ACT FIVE

Manacles for Judith's legs

Bed in cell

A stool

Jailor's lantern (could be replaced with a candle)

LIGHTING AND SOUND EFFECTS

A NOTE ON THE MUSIC

Lute music is indicated at opening, closing and act breaks; this is not essential to the performance, and can be cut, or replaced by alternatives, as required. Our lutenist, Sam Brown, selected appropriate Renaissance lute music from his repertoire for the original staged reading; I have given his choices here.

Opening lute music: Nicolas Vallet, *Pavan en Forme de Complainte.*

ACT ONE

Lights up: interior daylight.

Trumpet and drums.

Lights down.

Act break: John Danyel, excerpt from *Her Leaves Be Greene.*

ACT TWO

Lights up: exterior daylight.

Trumpets.

Tavern roar.

Lights down.

Act break: Robert Johnson, excerpt from *The Prince's Almain.*

ACT THREE

Lights up: exterior daylight at dawn – the light increases throughout the scene.

Trumpets and shouts.

Lights down.

Act break: John Dowland, excerpt from *Willoughby's Welcome Home.*

ACT FOUR

Lights up: interior daylight.

Banging at the door.

Trumpeting, banging of drums and clattering of boots.

Banging at the door.

Banging again.

Banging again.

Banging even louder.

Blackout.

Act break: John Danyel, excerpt from *Rosa*.

ACT FIVE

Lights up: interior moonlight.

Jailor's lantern (or candle) also gives light.

Egerton blows out the lantern. There is only moonlight.

Knocking.

Cockerel crows.

Bells chime.

Closing (from Judith's first 'Remember me'): Nicolas Vallet, *Pavan* (first section).

Blackout.

Music continues for a few moments, and then ceases.

Lightning Source UK Ltd.
Milton Keynes UK
UKOW06f0757100216

268073UK00001B/8/P